This Old House

This Old House

Poetic Expressions About Faith, Family, and Friends

Minnie Leonard

Old house, you were great, though so very small.
There was no other place for us, you were our all.
Cracks in the rooftop let stars peep through at night
And the first dawning of the bright morning light.

—This Old House, page 62

Dedication

I dedicate these poems to my mother who had a great love of writing, and stressed the importance of us memorizing poems. At Easter, Christmas, and family gatherings, we would recite poems that she taught us.

My mother was very strong in her mind, spirit, and actions. The mother of thirteen children, the wife of a Share Cropper with limited means, she had the ability to provide even when there was nothing available.

Through her example, we learned that whether we had little or much, we always had enough to share. Everyone was worthy of your love and respect, and your needs would be provided for regardless of your situation. Her life was a true example of her teachings.

Dedicated to my mother:
MAMIE LAWYER JONES (1911-1983)

Copyright © 2009 by Minnie Leonard
All rights reserved

Published by:
  John Davis Marshall Publishing
  PO Box 2136
  Stone Mountain GA 30086

Cover Design and Layout: Cathleen Kwas

Cover Photo: Christine Ambrose

ISBN: 978-0-9820475-9-0
Printed in the United States of America

This book or parts thereof may not be reproduced in any form, stored in a retrieval system, or transmitted in any form by any means—electronic, mechanical, photocopy, recording, or otherwise—without prior written permission of the publisher, except as provided by United States of America copyright law.

Table of Contents

Faith

I Am Free	2
God Never Fails	3
My Children	4
O' Man of God	5
A Good Man Steps Are Ordered by the Lord	7
The Aged – Some of Our Favorite People	8
Love	9
God Is …	11
My Feelings	12
Is It Really a Gloomy Day?	13
Why? Why? Why?	14
A Tribute to Our Sisters in Christ	16
Live, Love, Laugh	17
The Pattern for Living	18
Restoring the Royalty	19
Eternity	20
Thank You Lord	21

This Old House

A Servant of the Lord 22
The Joy of a Sister 23
My Sister, I Need You 24
Help Me Lord 25
My Preacher's Wife 26
True Friendship 27
Our First Lady 28
The Golden Rule 29

Family

"Mom's View, Dad's Too" 32
A Tribute to Mother 35
God Has Given Us a Servant 36
For My Brother-in-Law on His Retirement 37
A Lovely Couple 38
Our Family Tree 40
Our Family 41
A Tribute to Our Major ... Rosa L. Gaines 42
A Tribute from Your Sisters (for your retirement) 43
We Are Family 44
A Special Daughter 45
A Labor of Love 46
Who Is He? 47
Happy Birthday, Mom 49
Mother 50

Friends

Our Children	52
Happy Birthday My Love	54
Thanks to Our Teachers	55
Walking in Colum-bia	56
Don't Give Up	57
The Beauty of Nature	59
The Valley of Love	60
Bird Songs	61
This Old House	62
To Our Staff	63
On the Retirement of a Friend	64
Boys and Girls	65
Be Encouraged	66
America's Black Woman	67
A Friend to Friends	69
About the Author	71

Faith

*Praise the Lord; He called me by His grace
He gave me a pattern in the finest of
Spiritual taste...*

—*The Pattern for Living, page 18*

I Am Free

Thank you Lord, I am free
To be whatsoever you want me to be
A humble Servant, meek and mild
Free to endure temptation and trials

I am free to work, perform my task
Deeds of righteousness that will surely last
No not blind and laden with sin
A wonderful change has occurred within

Free from the burdens and loads of care
Fill with joy and peace I am free to share
I am free to love to share the Christ
To give all who will, saving advice

I am free to have peace as I suffer pain
Though misunderstood, it produces great gain

Yes, Yes, I am free.

Minnie Leonard

God Never Fails

After a long day of trials and tests
And many failures when I've done my best
I feel so lonely, like no one cares
In need of somebody my burdens to share.
Just for a chance to pour out my heart
Maybe consider a fresh start
My tears flow as from a fountain free
With the shaking of dry bones inside of me.

In your presence Lord, I will look up and pray
For only you will triumphantly get me through this day.
Life is full of stress and strains untold
Only faith and God's grace keeps my soul.

O for the joy of one good day
When pain and sorrows are rolled away
All my heaviness I know no more
My focus is on that eternal shore.

Finally, through my deep dark valley, I can see light
In the midst of it all my relief is in sight.
Praise the Lord, our God never fails
But we must stay within His vale.

This Old House

My Children

My children, my children
You are in God's love,
Protected and guarded by Jesus' blood.
He knows where you are, all the secret things
Comfort yourself in the joy and peace He brings.

When the days seem long and night so dark
There is hope and light in our heart.
We are assured we are never alone
Knowing through our faith, to whom we belong.

Thanksgiving and praise is always in order
Praise from every son and every daughter.
In all circumstances, God is pleased
When we praise His name, He sets our hearts at ease.

Minnie Leonard

O' Man of God

The first creation of human kind
Shaped and formed with God's hand divine
Courageous, strong, gentle, and brave
Yet made He Him from the dust of graves.

By His own will God made man
Commanded him His creation to sustain
How great God must think of you O' man
He gave you duties so noble and grand.

The head of the family he will become
To share, nurture, and keep every one…
From his wife to the youngest child
His example must be to lead and guide.

How great you are O' man of God
To keep His will you must work hard
Family fun and neighborly play
Must all be done to complete your day.

Now that the day is almost done
Comes the setting of the evening sun
O' man of God, gather the family around
All must come, it's now prayer time.

Thanksgiving, praise, and honor He gives
Praise with meditation and prayer as he daily lives.
O' man of God lead us in His will
That by His might, we will stand still.

This Old House

A daily walk with Him you know
Will lead us to that eternal shore
Where those who have gone on before
Are waiting for us at the heavenly door.

Minnie Leonard

A Good Man Steps Are Ordered by the Lord

We are very thankful you came our way.
You taught us to learn, grow, trust, and obey.
Though you were young and lacked many things,
With the love and support of friends,
You were successful just the same.

We see the evidence in the work you've done
Laboring night and day, from sun to sun.
Without a doubt,
Sometimes we knew you were tired
By your faith and determination,
You put away selfish pride.

Finally, after years of toiling, joys, sorrows, trials, and test,
We are assured; we've each received your best.
Any man may stumble, but we've never seen you fall,
For the steps of a good man are ordered by the Lord.

This Old House

The Aged – Some of Our Favorite People

You are our favorite brethren,
You have been with us so long;
Your body might have weakened,
But your faith has grown strong.

Your work of faith is seen,
By everyone who is here;
Your calm spirit and kindness
Bring our heart much cheer.

The example we see by way of actions,
Still fulfilling your duties from day-to-day
Encouraging the strong, nurturing the weak
Making sure we all stay in the right way.

A prayer of thanksgiving we utter to God,
As we pray in Jesus name,
That He will give us wisdom and courage
And that our examples may be the same.

Minnie Leonard

Love

*Love is strong like a mighty tower
Love is beautiful like a field of wild flowers.*

*Love is fragile, it can be destroyed
If its roots are not planted and hidden in God.*

*Love is plentiful and far reaching
As long as you use it, it's ever increasing.*

*Love is like a tiny flower, picked by a child,
To give to his mother with a big hug and smile.*

*Love is doing without necessity, to share with another
Whether it's your neighbor or maybe just your brother.*

*Love is greater than the sunlight which disappears by night
When others treat us wrong, love finds
joy in treating them right.*

*Love causes one to hurt and suffer many things
Love also brings comfort amidst all pain.*

*Love produces wisdom, though sometime unaware
Love promotes actions which show that we care.*

*Love is being fair and honest even when it hurts.
When this is our practice, we have Godly results.*

*Love is a mystery that can never be fully told.
When compared to others, it provides the strongest hold.*

This Old House

*The greatest act of love man has ever known
Is Christ giving His life to save us from all wrong.*

*Love never fails. It is the greatest of all.
Love is of God. In Him we cannot fall.*

*Love is very precious you see, my friend.
It is from the beginning and love never ends.*

Minnie Leonard

God Is …

God is my refuge from every storm of life.
God is my Savior, for He gave us the Christ.

God is my strength, a strong tower is He.
God is my life, for He lives in me.

God is my salvation, eternal life He gives.
To all who follow His footsteps and in Him daily live.

God is my light. In darkness I will not walk,
For His word is here to guide me;
There is power in His talk.

God is my all sufficiency,
In Him I have no need.
My heart is filled with thanksgiving.
For His grace and mercy I plead.

My Feelings

May I express to you from the start
It's not easy to convey what's in my heart.
Through your kindness of giving me a chance
With a few words, I will advance.

Now I am not my own, I've been bought with a price.
The precious blood of Jesus, the Christ.
Yes, I rejoice and praise Him too
Knowing what He has done for me and you.

Lord I am not what I desire to be
In the shadow of Your cross I am guilty you see.
Thank You for forgiveness, help me to take heed
As I walk Your pathway, for grace and mercy I plead.

Thank You for my family, who shares my joy and pain.
And for that victory banner, that is so heavily blood stained.
I can never praise You enough Lord, though I will try.
For even in my failure, You are always by my side.

Minnie Leonard

Is It Really a Gloomy Day?

Look around you: See the Son –
Not in the sky, but in everyone.
The gift of life that lives inside
Gives the brightest light like the ocean's tide.

The weather is gloomy; yes I can see
But the light of life is inside of me.
So let it shine, wherever we are,
Light the world like the moon and star.

A glowing countenance, a smiling face
For sure is evidence of God's grace.
Cast off the frown, put on a grin
With the indwelling light, we are sure to win.

Heads up! Listen up! Cheer up my friend!
The light of life dwells within.
Let's use what we have; shine our lights,
Then there's never a gloomy day or night.

Why? Why? Why?

Why, when a sister goes astray, it is so easy for us to say
What happened to her, I am surprised?
Well, that's the result of compromise.

Why didn't we help that sister in her distress?
Why didn't we lay her head upon our breast?
Why didn't we hurt and share her pain?
Tender love and care brings great gain.

Why when our older sisters give us advice
We are convinced they are wrong as we think twice?
These older sisters have not today's knowledge
How can they help me solve my problems?

Why do we say, "We know God's Word is Truth?"
And yet His commandment to obey our husbands
Blows our minds right through the roof?

Why do we call it being so rough?
Always bringing up old stuff?
Well, I guess you forgot my friend,
All disobedience is still sin.

Please, my sister, repent, start anew.
God will guide you in all you do.
Well, I will challenge us to the test
The way we live says it best.

Minnie Leonard

Why can't you see Christ on that cross?
With blood and water, flowing for the lost?
Can you not really see the Christ?
Then how can we ever compromise.

This Old House

A Tribute to Our Sisters in Christ

*We were so impressed with the activities last night
To share our feelings in writing just seemed right.
To all who participated, every smiling face
Displayed the evidence of God's amazing grace!*

*You gave us hope, courage, and joy for the day.
We know our love will continue in this way.
So Sisters, look up, smile up; enjoy God's beauty.
Service in love to each of us is our God-given duty.*

*To all the wonderful hard-working Sisters,
Especially of West Perrine –
Continue your labor of love in peace.
It is evidence of God's grace divine.*

Minnie Leonard

Live, Love, Laugh

Living places one in a perfect position to love
Loving makes the heart joyful,
Joy can produce abundant laughter
Can you imagine living without love and laughter?

Life came through sincere love.
Love is our great gift from above.
It is eternal, love never fails
Without it, there's no Gospel story to tell.

Laughter and love can be contagious
With results that extends through the ages.
Live, Love, Laugh, you can't go wrong!
Your life can become one happy song!

This Old House

The Pattern for Living

Praise the Lord; He called me by His grace
He gave me a pattern in the finest of
Spiritual taste.

He gave me many examples by way of sisters
Many very old.
By their wisdom, faithfulness, and love
And their spiritual joy untold.

Thank you Lord for saving me
I want to be a pattern too.
There are some, who are wayward,
Lord, I want to bring them back to you.

Help me to be a Pattern Lord
That others in me may see
Your loving kindness, grace, and mercy
And your blessed salvation free.

Minnie Leonard

Restoring the Royalty

My Brethren, we were alienated from the
Commonwealth of God
A sinful path we chose to trod.
We knew not the righteous way
All like sheep had gone astray.

But a price was paid on that old rugged Cross
Precious blood was shed to save the lost.
Through obedience of the Gospel of this great love,
Our souls are purified and sealed for above.

Now inside lives the Holy Spirit to guide,
No need to follow our sinful nature and pride.
We are a chosen generation, a Holy Nation,
A peculiar people who endure with Godly patience.

Lord of Lords, King of Kings
The precious one who changed our name
Take heed to yourself, restore your soul
Never forget this love Story of Old.

Eternity

Early in the morning before it was yet day
A heavenly light came to brighten my way
In an instant I was changed
To a new life, I will never be the same.

The former things are all behind
No pain, no labor, no ups and downs
Peace and joy will always be
For I am here for eternity.

So prepare yourself for that heavenly light
It may come morning, noon, or night
Walk upright and a good steward be
For in a flash, you will be in eternity.

Minnie Leonard

Thank You Lord

Thank you Lord for this day
You have kept us in your way
When our minds wandered astray
Your Spirit reminded us to pray.

Thank you Lord for giving your love,
So we can have a home above,
From all our suffering we can flee
To a home with Thee eternally.

Thank you Lord for a chance,
To live and learn, and our life enhance,
Through fellowship and prayer we can remember
Your life, so loving, kind and tender.

Thank you Lord for all you've done,
Giving us a Savior, your dear Son,
Continue our blessings, Lord we plead
Forgive our faults and supply our needs.

This Old House

A Servant of the Lord

Praise the Lord! I am His servant
Willing to do all that I can
Though sometimes it's ups and downs.
Yet through His strength, I stand.

I strive to be a good example
That the entire world might see
What a wonderful, wonderful change
The Holy Spirit has wrought in me.

My Master, I pray for wisdom
To perform my deeds and actions
There's no desire or lust in me
To be the center of attraction.

I will be a humble servant in my daily walk
Faithfully serving God through my fellowman
That my work may be seen, not just idle talk
This I pledge to keep to the end of my life span.

Minnie Leonard

The Joy of a Sister

When I think of you my heart lights up.
You must have been born with that beautiful smile
Your loving kindness leaves a mark on everyone you meet.
Without thinking, your words are soothing and comforting.
I don't know if you were a special order
But I know you are a special blessing.

When you correct me, tears of joy flow from my eyes,
As I move forward, I am so thankful you
Saved me from the error of my way.
That big gentle hug you give me,
O the love and peace I feel.

Truly you are the joy of a sister ...

My Sister, I Need You

When my head is low, and tears are falling
To my feet, I need you to lean on
When my heart is broken and my life is torn
Please, Sister, help me to be strong.

I do have a desire to pray
But there's so much trouble in my way
Can't utter a word, just sitting alone
Please Sister, sing for me a happy song.

Words of joy ringing in my ears,
Songs of praise for me to hear,
Will lift me up and give me hope
Thank you, Sister, for this antidote.

Smile for me Sister,
So glad you are here,
The comfort of your presence
Dry up my tears.

Minnie Leonard

Help Me Lord

Thank you Lord for this day
Keep me in your way I pray
Lord, I have not done all that I could
Sometimes I fail sometimes misunderstood.

Help me Lord to be brave and strong
And remember to whom I belong
I must be an example for all to see
That you, Lord, live inside of me.

I desire so much to uphold your name
Oh, I need courage I don't want to be ashamed
When I think of all you've done for me
I must live Holy and joyfully.

This Old House

My Preacher's Wife

M ...   Mother, keeper of the home, busy as a Bee
Y ...   Yet, your Servant as you can plainly see

P ...   Peacemaker, prayerful in God's will
R ...   Ready to share her talents and skills
E ...   Easy to work with whatever the task
A ...   Anchored in the Lord, whose strength will last
C ...   Caring, a quality we all must possess
H ...   Her hope in Christ keeps her doing her best
E ...   Echo His love both far and near
R ...   Reaching out to the lost with Godly fear
S ...   Savior keep her close we hold her dear

W ...   Wisdom is God's gift to my preacher's wife
I ...   Inner strength to solve confusion and strife
F ...   Faith to go where she has never been
E ...   Earnestly seeking to be saved in the end.

Minnie Leonard

True Friendship

T ...   Trust in God the greatest friend of all
R ...   Resist temptation great and small
U ...   Use the whole armor of God for Your Protection
E ...   Eternal life is ours in the resurrection

F ...   Friends work together, share everything
R ...   Reap the harvest that Godly obedience bring
I ...   In spirit and truth, live a life of peace
E ...   Endure the hardships there is sweet relief
N ...   Never turn back when burdens seem too hard
D ...   Dare you quit, this pathway we must trod
S ...   Savior, thank You, for You are always there
H ...   Happy are we Your presence to share
I ...   Indwelling Holy Spirit keep us strong and brave
P ...   Praising our true friend for He is willing to save.

Our First Lady

O ...   Oh the beauty of her spirit
U ...   United with Christ and her fellowman
R ...   Ready to serve wherever needed

F ...   Fervent charity for everyone
I ...   Involved in the work of the Lord
R ...   Resolved to stay the course for Christ
S ...   Seeking always the good for others.
T ...   Teaches by example

L ...   Love to share
A ...   Abundantly gives of herself
D ...   Diversity is her strength
Y ...   Yes, this is our first lady.

Minnie Leonard

The Golden Rule

The Lord has been so good to me.
He opened doors I could not see
When I didn't have shoes for my feet
Not so much as a warm place to sleep.

When those around me laughed and scorned
Because my clothes where old and torn
I must admit my feelings were hurt
By God's grace I didn't give up.

I was not valued by what I wore
Neither by all the pain I bore
The sun always shines after the rain
There is a divine cure for everything.

Along the way I grew strong
I learned my life was not my own
Prayers were uttered day and night
That I may faithfully treat others right.

Thank you Lord for mercy from above
Please help me show your matchless love
Hidden in my heart is your tool!
To live by the golden rule.

Family

*By the great wisdom of God above,
He made our family with care and love;
Showing kindness and concern for each other
For by His will, we are all brothers…*

Our Family, page 41

This Old House

"Mom's View, Dad's Too"

Our second child, a baby boy,
Warm and cuddly, a little bundle of joy.
Well this little bundle wasn't little very long,
Rapidly becoming physically and mentally strong!

As a young child, he was strong willed and loved to debate,
Give him an inch, and a mile he would take.
Through adolescence he was short and thin,
But not diminished; there was a way to fit in.

At eight years old, a little sister was born.
What a proud big brother, so caring and strong.
But to his older brother, Oh what a challenge,
Never let him win, even if it took a little malice.

From his youth up, he loved the older generation,
Who taught him about life, and how to handle temptation.
They seemed amazed sometimes, as he pricked their minds.
Wondering if he had left his childhood behind.

He dreamed of being a football star, living a luxurious life.
Sporting fancy cars, showing off a beautiful wife.
Now comes high school, look – he's beginning to grow!
Wearing those platform shoes and a very bushy "fro."
Quite a popular guy he is, and likes to look his best,
Wish he gave more attention to study,
preparing to pass his test.
Playing high school football, he thinks he's a star.
Flirting with all those cheerleaders, both near and far.

Minnie Leonard

Likes to bring home friends, and cook his special burgers,
Feeding friends and teammates, those fast food lovers.
Busy with high school life, Oh! To him it's such fun,
Little did he know, so soon it would be done.

Well, now it's off to college, to a school out of town,
Just a little unhappy, to leave his sweetheart behind.
Guess what? Two years later, he is at the altar
Making vows with his high school sweetheart to never falter.

What a young man! Grown up, matured he thinks,
A prayer dear Lord is, please don't let him sink.
They seemed so very happy, nothing could pull them apart.
But this is not unusual, this is just the start.

His brother and sister, Dad and I are all happy too.
As well wishes came forth from everyone of you.
No more our little boy, we respect you as a man,
With your own family to lead, with God you must stand.

A wayward faith we saw in his actions
For sure, God was not the center of attraction.
Sorry, my son, this will bring trouble,
Although now you seem as happy as a bubble.

A few years later, my prediction came true.
There were so many problems; he didn't know what to do.
Our God is merciful; He worked it out for good,
Now he declares, God's word must be understood.

What a change of heart God has wrought,
Now, he understands all the things we taught.
The fruit of the spirit began to arise,
A once wayward son now leads his wife to Christ.

This Old House

Having children of their own to nurture and bring to God,
Teaching them how to live and in God's way to trod.
As his parents and his first teacher
We had no idea he would someday become a preacher!

Spreading the Good News, the Gospel of Christ
Deep inside, we praise the Lord for our second child.

Love you, ... Mom and Dad

Minnie Leonard

A Tribute to Mother

*Our first memories of mother when we were small
She was truly the greatest of them all
Very loving and caring, sometimes she spanked
For all of her nurturing to God we give thanks.*

*As we grew and developed through the years
There were times we brought her many tears.
But she continued to love us and mold our lives
Her hope and prayer was for us to live for Christ.*

*Though you are gone, you are still very near
Your pleasant memories brings us good cheer
Your love and tender care will never depart
There's a special place for you in each of our hearts.*

This Old House

Written to my son ...
God Has Given Us a Servant

Great men come and great men go
Some of whom we've heard of, some we personally know.
Some have left monuments, noting their time in history
Looked up to by their peers
Who thought their works a mystery.

Great men have lived and walked the shores of time
With many noble accomplishments, all left behind.
These things are wonderful and noteworthy, my friend.
Our sojourn here is limited, so soon it must end.

But you my son must be greater than these
With a life of humility and servitude,
Your master will be pleased.
Laboring daily with gentleness and love
Will show that your wisdom is from above.

You may be looked down upon, and frowned upon by men.
In God's own time, this too will end.
So be God's great man, a servant, if you will.
Work in His vineyard and your life will be fulfilled.

In you, my son, God has given us a servant.
Love, Mom

Minnie Leonard

For My Brother-in-Law on His Retirement— April 20, 1996

Up in the morning before the crack of dawn
You must be ready for work by the peep of the sun.
Praying and hoping for a better day
Believing in your heart, "It will come my way."

In the course of time, that dream came true.
For at the workplace, there were many new things to do.
Weaving in and out around the city
As you drove their truck,
Seemed much easier, but still tedious work.

After many years experience and faithful work,
A position became available to relieve you of the old truck.
An inside job, an office, a desk,
But you didn't build your hopes up, you knew it wasn't rest.

Profitable to your company, you have always been –
Formulating ideas, following new trends.
Helping others to learn, mature, and strive
Using your wisdom to help others become wise.

The task has proven you a brave and strong man,
When called to duty, willing and able to stand.
You have worked hard for a long time ---
Now comes the privilege to sit, settle, and unwind.

A Lovely Couple

Today, we go beyond our custom,
We honor our oldest sister and her husband;
As a gift to us, they are one of God's blessings,
For from them, we've learned many lessons.

They are always warm and willing to share
All the bountiful meals she cooks with loving care;
Plenty to eat seems to be her trait,
No wonder we are all a little overweight.

When we first met our brother-in-law,
He was tall, handsome, and skinny as a straw;
With high cheek bones and deep set eyes,
So warm and friendly with a charming smile.

From the very beginning he fitted right in,
Accepted our family, a new found friend.
We believed he loved us; at least we thought,
And did appreciate the joy he brought.

Through years of marriage, he's good to her,
Always there when a need did occur,
A persistent hard worker, sometimes day and night,
To provide for his family, even when things are tight.

They gave to their children above request,
Never satisfied until they had the best.
Rearing their family has had its fill of
love and joy and many tears.

Minnie Leonard

Time has passed, the children are gone
Leaving only the two of you at home;
Enjoy each other, make every moment worthwhile,
Increase your life in a Godly style.

We love you, our sister and our brother,
Think it's wonderful you found each other,
The events of this day, we hope you will treasure,
Now may you go forward in peace and pleasure.

This Old House

Our Family Tree

We are so happy, as you can see
For all the offspring of our family tree.
Many have moved, or chosen to roam;
What a blessing it is when you return home.

For the family feast, the joy, the fun;
Enjoy the fruit of our labor from the work we've done.
Many times throughout the year we fail to see
The numerous talents and abilities in our family.

We share our energies, we teach, we learn;
Our family growth shows what we've done.
Every branch of the tree must do its part
For the outward activities show what's in the heart.

To our fore parents who worked hard all their days
For the love of our family, you are worthy of praise.
Let us never forget from where we came
And all the great memories our fore parents bring.

Minnie Leonard

Our Family

*By the great wisdom of God above,
He made our family with care and love;
Showing kindness and concern for each other
For by His will, we are all brothers.*

*We will rejoice together and share our feelings,
When mistakes are made, our hearts are forgiving.
How beautiful to see what God has done!
Our family is His gift, nothing we've earned.*

*From our fore parents to this present generation,
We are specially made by His creation.
So wonderful to see your smiling face
Exemplifying the gift of our Lord's grace!*

*As our family continues to love and grow,
To share our joy and our woes,
Treat each other with kindness and gently care,
Assuring our fellowship throughout the year.*

A Tribute to Our Major …
Rosa L. Gaines

It takes a very special person you see
To diligently serve this great nation.
Our people, our lands, and everything therein,
From our Chief Executive to our foes and friends.

Dedicated, working day and night tirelessly,
Around the world for the brave and the free,
As this chapter of your life settles down to the dust
There will always be memories of what you've done for us.

The many accomplishments and hard earned victories
Are now engraved parts of our great history
May God keep you in His love, grace, mercy, and peace
And continued freedom to serve from the greatest to the least.

We love you,
Your entire family

Minnie Leonard

A Tribute from Your Sisters
(For your retirement)

Hey up there, will you come down,
Girl, you must feel like you are on cloud nine
Today you are special, you are retired!!!
As sisters we are so very proud.

No more up in the morning and work all day.
You now have time for fun and play.
Now we are not offering you breakfast in bed,
No reason to be lazy, stay active instead.

You have accomplished the goals of your dreams
Through years of hard work
And planning and schemes
Now it's time for the sisters' wish for you
Eat, drink, and be happy in whatever you do!

We Are Family

As a very lively growing tree, with many branches,
Present and past
Dear Lord, please bless this family to last.

We come in many shades, shapes, and sizes,
All different, but yet in style.
When all together we do our best
Sure we can win, no matter what the test.

About as diverse as plants in a field
Proud as Georgia Pines on a tall hill.
Yet we are humble, we help each other
We know we are family.

Thank you Lord for this family
A strong, growing, lively tree.
We appreciate the fun, laughter, stress and strain.
Thank you Lord for everything.

Minnie Leonard

A Special Daughter

Of the little girls in heaven above,
In God's great wisdom and His love –
A special blessing for me to share,
He gave me a daughter who loves and cares.

Fulfilling His promise, He gave my desire.
He gave me a daughter, a special child,
The privilege to love, teach, train, and guide
With Godly fear and unselfish pride.

He let me live to see you learn and grow,
And pass the stages through which a child must go.
Through trembling and fear we prayed each day,
That with trials and errors,
You would find the way.

From a humble beginning, a tiny seed,
You've grown and blossomed
Like a flowering weed.
May you have the blessings someday I plead,
Of a daughter of your own from a tiny seed.

This Old House

A Labor of Love
(Written for Mrs. Grace Adams upon her retirement from caring for children in her home.)

We have seen your loving care in so many ways.
Our memories are ever present of your long enduring days.

Parents and children alike, you took us all in
Sharing your possessions and kindness as a good friend.

Physically and spiritually, you fed our little ones
Giving constant attention until the day was done.

Our little children, you gently shaped and molded.
Though there were times when it was necessary to scold.

Thank you for so many years of ups and downs
Nurturing children from all around.

Through it all,
You remained a great wife, mother, and friend.
Our love and great thoughts of you will never end.

Minnie Leonard

Who Is He?

*Gentle, kind, always caring;
His greatest joy comes from sharing.*

*Genuine concern for those he knows
Without second thought, if needed he goes.*

*A very hard worker, he has always been,
To earn an honest living without the lust of sin.*

*Work his regular job, do your plumbing, clean your yard;
If a dollar is involved, for him it's not too hard.*

*He plays the harmonica, likes to have fun,
Even when a long hard day is done.*

*A good man is he, yet made many errors,
With his growing wisdom, saves many from terror.*

*With reverence for God, he has developed through the years.
To learn of his past often brings tears.*

*The oldest of thirteen, he had little chance for education;
Yet, has earned a good living
Through hard work, and dedication.*

*Concerned and obedient even as a child,
His unique way of living brought his parents many smiles.*

*Even though our parents are with us no more,
He tries with every effort to keep unity and love aglow.*

This Old House

Now with thirteen children of his own,
An example he tries to be,
Through his life of toiling and labor
They know a living does not come free.

Who is this special man?
He has to be one or the other,
Puzzle your brain no longer; he is our oldest brother.

Minnie Leonard

Happy Birthday, Mom

*To our mother, our friend, our gift from God.
For all that we are, you have worked very hard.
Never wavering a moment, when we are sick or well,
How you managed the pace, only God can tell.*

*We are not always obedient, how well you know
If we told the truth or a lie, our face will always show.
Sometimes we wonder how you became so smart.
You seem to know our secrets, even what's in our hearts.*

*Through the years, you have given ... never asked for any pay.
Finally, Mom, we've chosen this to be your special day
To show our gratitude and to put our love into action,
For this grand occasion, you are the center of attraction.*

*So enjoy yourself with family and friends.
May the joy and memories never end.
You deserve much more; we can never repay.
But from our hearts, we wish you a …. Happy Birthday!!*

Mother

The wonderful touch of a loving Mother
Can't be compared to any other;
How blessed to have had her so many years;
Living without her often brings tears.

Never take for granted ... Mother,
That great gift God gave.
For there is an empty space in life
When she is in the grave.

Rejoice, be glad, and enjoy her touch.
She is God's gift to you.
Her love guides,
And her strength provides
Leadership for all we do.

Friends

Valley of love, Oh valley of love
There are so many hugs
In the valley of love!

—The Valley of Love, page 60

This Old House

Our Children

Thank you Lord for our little ones,
The greatest gifts under the sun,
Wiggle, giggle, crawl, and walk.
Not too long before they learn to talk.

Outside playing, they've learned to run,
Into one thing or another from dust to dawn,
Our little children grow up so fast,
Wish this childhood stage could last.

Learning to listen and follow the rules,
The lessons of behavior, working 'n school.
Our little children grow up so fast,
Wish this childhood stage could last.

Into adolescence, then teenage life,
Putting into practice what they learned about Christ.
How to stand firm when pressured by peers,
Even though resisting sometime brings tears.

Beautiful young ladies, strong young men,
Following our footsteps as life recommends.
Heed to our life we take day by day,
So our examples won't lead them astray.
It's time to date, bring home new friends,
They seem so happy, laughing never ends.
Be careful of your choice, we often warn,
We share their joy with deep concern.

Minnie Leonard

When things don't go right they wish we understood
And always be there, as good parent should.
Frequently, we advise them, "Honey, take time and pray."
They'd like to have us listen, with much less to say.

Our challenge seems greater as our children grow up,
Thank you Lord for our blessings, we know it's not luck.
To see them mature in grace and knowledge,
The ways of the world they learn to abolish.

Time moves on, now they are grown,
Though many times our hearts were torn,
How thankful we are, we stayed together,
Helped them through life's stormy weather.

Thank you Lord, for giving them to us,
Our sons and daughters – to parents you entrust
Every child you give is truly a blessing,
They help us mature in all of life's lessons.

This Old House

Happy Birthday My Love

With each passing year, each Birthday
You are more adorable, charming,
And, of course, more of what my heart desires.

All the events of our lives
Every milestone we have celebrated together
Reminds me of your endurance, your strength
No matter what we have had to weather.

Of the many words in our language
There's none suitable to express
The depth of my love, the magic in my heart,
But I will give it my best.

You are truly the Greatest!
Happy Birthday my love!

Minnie Leonard

Thanks to Our Teachers

Our teachers show that working
With children can be fun –
Helping and guiding them as they learn.
You meet the challenge, utilizing all the necessary skills
From channeling their thoughts aright,
To cleaning up spills.

We can never thank you enough for all that you do
In preparing our little one's minds for future use.
Hats off to all! A job well done!
Your works will be remembered through them
In years to come.

This Old House

Walking in Colum-bia

*Walking in Colum-bia is great fun
Walking in Colum-bia in the early morning sun.*

*Picking pretty wild flowers all along the way
One can spend many hours in the course of a day.*

*The natural beauty ... the lovely trees
The still quietness ... the early morning breeze.*

*Thoughts can run a mile a minute
One can walk, put everything in it.
The silent calmness in the breeze makes one feel so at ease.*

Minnie Leonard

Don't Give Up

*When you feel you are down and out,
Don't give up.*

*When there seems to be no rest in sight,
Don't give up.*

*When the sunshine has disappeared from your life,
Don't give up.*

*When your day is filled with anger and strife,
Don't give up.*

*If your family and friends turn you down,
Don't give up.*

*When the world seems to greet you with a frown,
Don't give up.*

*Our Heavenly Father still cares for you.
Don't give up.*

*Just by chance, try something new
Don't give up.*

*There is one in the heavenly realm,
Don't give up.*

*He will change your life if you just give it to Him.
Don't give up.*

This Old House

So praise the Lord, let Him fill your cup.
Life is worth living,
Don't give up.

Minnie Leonard

The Beauty of Nature

The sparkling green grass that glitters after the rain
The beautiful melody of many birds as they sing
Everything in its place, for its time, its work, and its season
Nothing is out of order being formed for a perfect reason.

The morning clouds are passing over
Bringing forth skies tinted blue
That the Master's artist has painted
with a brush of heavenly hue.

I observed the little ant, as busy as can be,
He has no permanent dwelling, his life is short you see.
He builds a mound, it is torn down;
He just can't seem to win.
But what a determined creature, he works unto the end.

Have you noticed the trees with their
many thousand of leaves.
How they give up their clothing at the first winter sneeze.
They seem to fall asleep, for a long rest is due.
They have provided a haven for the birds,
bees, and other creatures too.

This Old House

The Valley of Love

*Smiling faces picking daises
Voices unknown, singing songs
All in the valley of love!*

*The sun shines bright, the moon lights
The night,
The calm breeze, the peace, the ease,
All in the valley of love!*

*The winding streams, the trees towering,
The blooming flowers
All in the valley of love!*

*Animals grazing, people praising,
No sad times, happiness all around
All in the valley of love!*

*Valley of love, Oh valley of love
There are so many hugs
In the valley of love!*

Minnie Leonard

Bird Songs

The birds are singing a happy song
With voices so brave and strong.
Praises ring out in unspoken words
Expressing their joy and their love.

The trees are laden with birds of different kinds;
Their music rings out all around.
What a song, what a song they so happily sing.
Joy to my heart, they always bring.

This Old House

From my dad, my mom, and all my siblings ...
Your walls were bursting with love
Though so helpless, and so many needs
We were watched over and supplied from that
Great storehouse above.

So many people with so little space
All crammed within your walls.
Much contentment, lots of thanksgiving
Not much complaining at all.

The lessons we learned are unforgettable
Far greater than those written in books.
Without formal education, just simple wisdom,
My parents seemed to have known what it took.

We were trained to love each other, share everything.
Work hard and play together;
Good times, hard times, with or without,
We could make it through life's stormy weather.

Old house, you were great, though so very small.
There was no other place for us, you were our all.
Cracks in the rooftop let stars peep through at night
And the first dawning of the bright morning light.

We longed for years to see you again,
You are one of our most valued friends.
Like the little old church with no steeple –
You will live forever because of so many caring people.

Minnie Leonard

To Our Staff

*It is nice to have a day sometime to stop,
think, exercise our minds,
To see if anyone we pass
Had a good impression of us to last.*

*Just a moment to pause and think,
Might capture a mind that was on the blank,
To sort things out – put them in perspective
When we are back at work, we are more effective.*

*It's not bad to have a day of calm,
To share our thoughts, fold our arms.
To view the halls, watch people come and go
Offer service to those who need help through the door.*

*Hope you agree with what you've read
There is much more we could have said,
The idea of having a day sometime
To stop, think, and exercise our minds.*

On the Retirement of a Friend
(April 16, 1999)

There comes a time in every organization when the
Chain of love and care must be broken.
Your care and memories are planted in our hearts,
And we hope ours in yours,
With the love of this little token.

Your quiet walk and gentle voice, and of course,
That little quick dance step
Without a chance to know you well,
One could hardly imagine you had so much pep.

Oh, how your link will be missed as an
Intricate part of this great chain.
So please return soon and often
With that great smile you always bring!

Minnie Leonard

Boys and Girls

Boys and girls have happy faces,
Boys and girls like to go places.

Boys and girls like to work and play,
They will keep you busy all the day.

Boys and girls create things that are beautiful,
They will finish their task and they are dutiful.

Boys and girls are fun to be around,
What an excellent way to spend your time.

We make many new things, we share with friends,
Wish these good times would never end.

When the day is over, they are still going strong,
But as for me, I need to be alone.

To meditate, give thanks for a day well done,
For working with boys and girls is great fun.

Be Encouraged

*It is amazing what one can do
With continued effort and trust in God, too.
Through faith, hope, and endless stride
Many accomplishments can make one proud.*

*Never give up or find reason for despair,
Just remember there's always someone who cares.
In the midst of opposition, please take courage,
The harder you work the more you flourish.*

*There's a higher goal to be reached
Your life itself is a lesson, you teach
Continue to press forward, give it your best,
True victory comes through nothing less.*

Minnie Leonard

America's Black Woman

History tells me I came over on a boat
Without my consent I was set a float
During that turbulent journey from Africa
Many lives were lost
On that old rugged boat
As we were turned and tossed.

The survivors who reached America
Were sold as slaves.
We had no choice but to try and be brave
Couldn't speak the language
Beaten when we didn't understand
Expected to live and function in this strange land.

Forced to work hard, day and night
To build this great country with our strength and might
Often burdened and discouraged
But we took it in stride
A little voice inside of me would whisper
"Only the strong will survive."

Many of our husbands and sons were taken away
Never to return, no, not until this day
What a predicament to find ourselves in
No family core, not allowed to make friends.

Oh the pain, the woe, and the tears I shed
But it took courage; I had to be strong instead
That's when I learned there is a God

This Old House

Though I knew Him not then
I was always in the presence of an invisible friend
He gave me strength, lifted my soul
No matter how often I was beaten and scold.

Over the course of time, there was great change
I saw my future, my hope, my fame
However, life has been a struggle I must admit
Since arriving in America on that old slave ship.

I am still a pretty good pick among the chicks
A moving child who likes her clothes in the latest style
When I walk, I still jar the ground
About sixteen inches all around.

I am America's black woman!

Minnie Leonard

A Friend to Friends

*About the year Nineteen Hundred and Sixty-Six
I saw our country in somewhat of a fix.
Our Supreme Court ordered desegregation in the work place,
With this decision an opportunity stared me in the face.*

*A place to work I sought to find
Somewhere to increase my knowledge I had in mind.
To work with others and share my time
A special place, I wanted to stay around.*

*My work place gave me that chance – It was great,
A challenge it was, I felt that all I had was at stake.
Yes, there were many obstacles great and small,
But with God and you, we conquered them all.*

*Through the years, I've made many wonderful friends
My pleasant memories shall never end.
I appreciate my opportunity to work and earn a living,
To share with you my small givings.*

*My thanks to all of you for sharing my joys and tears,
You were always there throughout the years.
It's a little hard to say I must leave,
But, there is a place in my heart for each of you to cleave.*

About the Author

Minnie L. Jones Leonard was born near Tallahassee, Florida, in rural Leon County. She is the daughter of the late Mr. and Mrs. Alonzo Jones, and the eighth of fifteen siblings. She was married to the late John W. Leonard for forty-one years, and together they have three children, who have blessed her with four beautiful grandchildren. Mrs. Leonard is a retired Licensed Practical Nurse, who spends much of her time enjoying her hobbies, one of which is writing poetry. Her desire is that all readers will find a measure of inspiration, joy, and fulfillment in her poetry.